It is with the fingers of Love that we touch the beauty of life.

K. Vasanti

R1-00
49

Journey: A Compilation of Love Poems

by

Kasanti™

Bloomington, IN authorHOUSE™ Milton Keynes, UK

AuthorHouse™
1663 Liberty Drive, Suite 200
Bloomington, IN 47403
www.authorhouse.com
Phone: 1-800-839-8640

AuthorHouse™ UK Ltd.
500 Avebury Boulevard
Central Milton Keynes, MK9 2BE
www.authorhouse.co.uk
Phone: 08001974150

© *2006 Kasanti™. All rights reserved.*

No part of this book may be reproduced, stored in a retrieval system, or transmitted by any means without the written permission of the author.

First published by AuthorHouse 2/14/2006

ISBN: 1-4259-1176-5 (e)
ISBN: 1-4259-1175-7 (sc)

Library of Congress Control Number: 2005911337

Printed in the United States of America
Bloomington, Indiana

This book is printed on acid-free paper.

Table of Contents

Across the Waves 1

A Stone 2

Behold 4

Blue Butterflies 5

Breathless 6

Calm Restless Mind 7

Celeste 8

Cracked Pomegranate 9

Crying Stones 10

Cup of Tea 11

Deep within My Veins 12

Drops from My Heart 13

For You 14

Gentle Word 15

How can I? 16

How Long 17

How to Love 18

I Dare Not Say 19

I Feel You 20

If I 22

If You Cut Me 23

I Hope That You Remember 24

I Know You 25

I Miss You 26

Into the Night 27

I Think of You 28

I Thought Of You Today 29

I Want to Find a Way 30

Journey 32

Kiss Me 33

Last Kiss 34

Last Night 35

Let it Go 36

Like A Mist 37

Looking for You 38

Love's Fire 39

My Lady 40

Next Time 41

Morning Tea 42

Mundane Things 43

My Anchor 44

My Treasures 45

One Goodbye 46

One Song	47
One Thought	48
Release Me	49
Returning Home	50
Right Now	51
Satin Sheets	53
Second Skin	54
Shattered Innocence	55
Show Me the Face	56
Silent Waves	57
Small Diamond	58
Soft as the Night	59
Speak Softly	60
Still I Go On	61
Stillness of Your Voice	62
Still Standing	63
Stolen Kiss	64
Surrender	65
Ten Thousand Years	66
Thank You	67
The Fire	69
The Dance	70

The Parting 71
The Touch 72
This Beautiful Moon 73
Together Forever 74
Two Lovers 75
Unbroken Wall 76
Unspoken Words 77
What Might Have Been 78
Words 79
Yesterday 80
You Don't Have To 82

Across the Waves

My thoughts
Reach out to you across the waves
And gently caress your face.
From distant mountain tops
To the reaches of infinite space
Like the first kiss
Left in a glass of old wine.
The taste of your lips
Are sweeter with time.
I savor your fragrance
Which hangs in the air
Like curtains of freshness
After a shower of rain.
That soft spot behind your ear,
If you look closely
You'll find me resting there.
Across these mighty waves
I come
Though we are far apart
You will always know
That you are strong in my heart.

A Stone

Before me you stand,
With that enigmatic smile.
This will not be painful,
It's only for a while.
And like a practiced surgeon,
Without anesthetic or knife
You calmly stand before me,
And devastate my life.
With slashing verbs and clawlike words.
You rip apart my heart.
My crying voice cannot be heard.
My life now falls apart.
You place me in the balances,
Of scales which others have done.
Had I but known that this was to be the case,
Then it would've been better not to have begun.
I am left alone in the darkness,
Like a blind man catching straws.
Life experiences give us toughness.
But culture has her laws.
I have no magic portion,
To try and change your mind.
The stars are out of alignment.
Perhaps in another life, or another time.
You cast your words like a magic spell,
And turn me into stone.
I'm covered by an encrusted shell,
Forever to be alone.
The blood which rushes within my veins,
And animate this frame.

Lies in a crimson frozen pool,
Soon nothing will remain.
I am left with a little memory,
And thought of you and me,
I'll indulge in childlike fantasy,
Of that which might have been.

Behold

No thought
To hide
My nakedness.
No tears
To wash away
No words
To spread upon
The table
Of my heart
I stand
Before you
Naked
No fear
To cover
My soul
I lay bare
Before you
Open your heart
And
Behold

Blue Butterflies

Leaves play in the wind
Like blue butterflies in spring.
Twisting their stems around,
Before falling to ground,
To complete the eternal cycle.
But no! not today.
This scene we will delay,
Until another time.
For here beneath this canopied bough,
Lost between then and now.
I dwell in the thought of you.
From behind an iron mask,
This question you ask,
Will I love you forever,
How can I tell,
For the passion still swell
And I will leave you never.
The conflict which forms,
Between established norms.
Of love, duty and reason.
The path of life,
Though filled with struggle and strife,
Is the template on which we rise.
To ride on the wing,
Of the birds as they sing.
Is truly the path of the wise.
I follow the path,
Of blue butterflies as they laugh,
And rejoice to be in their company.

Breathless

Holding you in burning arms
Upon a bed of bleeding Roses
And you leave me Breathless.

Cold night, no sound, no sight
A slow burning touch
And still I am Breathless

Warm lips pressed breath to breath
No pulse or beating heart
Laying here with you, Breathless.

Lovers kiss, swirling mist
Two hearts within one soul
One life, one love, only the Breathless.

Fly away, another day
Sacred dew flowing down
Golden bowl, burning flame, Breathless.

Calm Restless Mind

I thought of many words to say
And hope to see your face today.
It might be strange to me, but true,
That I lose a day,
When I don't see you.
You make my spirits soar,
My heart rejoice.
My mind is ensnared
In the timbre of your voice.
Ten thousand times I call your name,
The silent reply, remains the same.
I sought you at the rainbow's end,
Sometimes as lover, but most times as friend.
After all of this searching,
One day I wish I'd find,
The still clear calm
Of my restless mind.

Celeste

There she sat, serene in beauty
Pictured in stately elegance
A shimmering star
Pulsing with a warm glowing light
When she moves it is like a brook
Whose waters lap lovingly
Against moss-covered silky stones
Her smile is as radiant
As the gold in the morning sun
Oh how I wish that I could tell you
Of the jade in the blue-green sea
Or of the silver in the eagle's eye.
My tongue is slow to speak
Of the passion which enflames my soul
Or of the dark and hungry longing
For you.
But I know that patience is nature's handmaiden.
And it is far better to drink.
From an empty cup, than become drunk
On too much spirit.
That I have had this chance to love you
Even though from afar is enough
For even in this day
Angels occasionally walk on the ground

Cracked Pomegranate

Blue butterflies float
From heart to heart.
Words spoken in love
Tied by the chains of duty.
Tears from soft brown eyes
In sobbing torrents falling
On the ground.
Cracked pomegranate
Pour out seeds of life.
Down the hill they roll
Head over heel.
Laughing at the play of gravity.
The world spins.
First earth then sky.
And I am lost among the planets
Like an errant child.
Throwing marbles into the ring of fate.
What's to become of those?
Sparks which fly
When the hammer falls.
Will they run like tachyons?
Through the barriers
Of space and time.
So much and yet so small.
A grain of sand
I hold in my hand
And all the world stood still

Crying Stones

You have taught me,
That love is strong.
But duty is stronger.
That time is eternal,
But tears last longer.
That wounds are deep,
But scars run deeper.
That a taste of life
Is better than all of life.
That content is useless,
We should only look at the frame.
Better it is not to start,
Than to burn with life's rage?
Or to use my iron will,
While living in my cage.
That freedom flies on wings of time.
Surely wisdom is the province of the wise.
There is no need for me to care,
It can all be explained away.
So, the hammer falls,
On stones and walls.
Causing sparks to fly.
Tears from my eyes begin to crawl.
Red rain falls from the sky.
Perhaps by now, I think you'll know,
That there is nothing really to show.
For stones at times are known to cry.
Perhaps this might be the reason why.

Cup of Tea

Morning splashed across the sky
As I turn in my bed
My thoughts gently caress you.
I follow the contours of your face.
And feel with my fingers
The smile at the corners of your mouth.
Is like the silver on the lake
In early spring as it dances with the sunlight.
Leaves waltzing between light and shade
And you here with me.
There is tea in the cup
As the mist slowly rise wafting
Its way to me.
Ah! Cinnamon, cherry or earl of grey
First light, second sight
New day.

Deep within My Veins

Strange,
That I should feel you
Stirring within my veins,
Centered in my marrow
Falling like inner rain
Rising from the deep
Like a dragon
Awaken from its sleep.
Heart and lung
Singing the same song
Beating in my chest
Like an old village drum.
Breath in, life out
Whether in silent whisper
Or in resounding shout
It's the same tide which rushes inside.
Pulling waves to the shore.
The blood in my veins
Is still the same
As the waves rushing to the shore.

Drops from My Heart

Tears well up in your eyes
And gently flow
Over the precipice
Of your eye lids.
While you sobbed
Drops of black blood
Fall from my heart
To burst into flames
As your tears
Touched the ground
If, if you would
Stay the torrent
Of your tears
Then my heart
Will cease to bleed

For You

I have abandoned all others,
For you.
Left my home and family,
For you.
Taken a great gulp of reality,
For you.
Swallowed my pride,
For you.
Searched deep inside,
For you.
Although I tried to hide,
From you.
Every where I went,
There was you.
There is no place,
Which does not reflect,
Some part of you.
For everywhere,
I go
There will always be you.

Gentle Word

If,
There were but one word
Which I could speak to you
That word would softly capture
Morning coming into view

If,
Time is short
And life was long.
And my heart could still hear
The silence in the song
Then maybe, just maybe
I would find this word
To gently speak to you.

How can I?

How can I express?
The Inexpressible,
Or listen to the inaudible.
When the medium is only words.
For what are words?
But phantoms flowing,
Across reeds in the mind.
Tracing strange melodies,
Upon tables of virgin sand.
Love is not an act,
But is a process, which passes,
Throughout life.
No beginning, no end.
When did love first begin?
There has never been a time
When I did not love you.
Come that time never when I will not.

How Long

Tell me how long is love
Perhaps,
Love is longer than
Tomorrow
Stretches further
Than the spider's web
Catches more
Than the upturned bowl
Or the sky
Perhaps,
It is sweeter than
The morning ray of sunshine
Shining so bright
That its light can not be seen
But only felt by the tip of fingers
Love transcends
Space and mind
Yet moves freely
Between the crevices
Of yesterday and today
Perhaps
Love is the glue
Which fixes us fast
In the here and now
In this moment
Within this thin segment
Of reality.
Perhaps
This is all we have
Perhaps all of this is
Love

How to Love

When you fall in love,
Fall with no thought at all
As to how, or where you will land.
For the joy of falling in love,
At least once in your lifetime.
Is worth the pain,
Of a thousand goodbyes.
The ecstasy of the anguish,
Wrung from a broken heart.
Though bitter to the taste,
Is like syrup to the soul.
And through the ache of your heart
You will come to know.
That despite the thorns,
The rose of love will grow.
And though your labor be long
It is at the altar of sacrifice
Where Love's weakness will be made strong.
So love with the same force
Which binds the planets together.
And cause the seedling.
To burst forth
From the womb of the earth
And when unrequited is your love.
Love still, knowing that,
There is no greater force,
In heaven above or below on earth.
There is no other way,
But to love now, love today.
For love is the glue,
Which sums up the whole,
And all of its parts.

I Dare Not Say

If only
I had the nerve
These are the words
I would say.

If only
I had the courage
I would take your hand
As my fears melt away.

If only
I had the strength
Then my hesitation of yesterday
Would not be repeated today.
But as you can see
I need
Voice, courage, strength
To simply say
I love you
So sad, that I can write
Yet, I dare not say.

I Feel You

I feel you
I feel
You
I feel you
Moving
Deep within
The spaces
Of my soul.
I feel you
Flowing
From thirsty deserts
To verdant
Flood plains
Drowning stalks
Of slender rice and weeds.
I feel you
Naked
Upon the cheeks
Of my unshaven face.
I feel you
Roar through
The bellows of my lungs.
I feel you
As blood
Flow through
Encrusted, calcified
Pipes.
I feel you
As I enter you
And you me

I feel you
I
Feel
You

If I

If I were to fall,
Would you give me your hand?
If my body became broken with pain,
Would you send me to my fathers?
If in my darkest hour,
Would you forsake yourself for me?
If death came for one of us,
Would you go and leave me?
If I went stumbling into the night,
Would you bring a light to find me?
My love, these things I ask of you now,
For there might come a time,
When you will have to respond,
Without me having to ask.

If You Cut Me

If you cut me, I will not bleed,
Stab me in the heart
I will not feel,
For you can no longer hurt me.
It was not so long ago,
That what you did affected me so.
But you have drawn so much from me,
That now it makes no difference you see.
For it was only yesterday,
When the thought of you
Could brighten my day.
But how could it be
That in so short a time,
The thought of you
Leaves splinters in my mind.
You have driven me beyond all pain
That I see life with indifference,
Whether it is sun or rain.
You have changed my smiling face,
Now life has only a bitter taste.
Dead is what I have become
Cold, encrusted, hollow and numb.

I Hope That You Remember

I hope that you
Remember me
Now that the love
Is gone
I hope that you
Remember me
You left me
So alone
I hope that you
Remember me
You left me standing here
I hope that you
Remember me
You never shed
A tear.

I Know You

You held your face to the sun
And was kissed by the light
Oh how I wished that I
Could be that light
For I know you
I have known you
From a time when time was not
I have swam through
Oceans of existences,
Through so many lives
So many forms
To find you
I know you
With the power
Of lightning as it strikes
The dormant seed
Deep in the bowels of the earth
I know you
As the sweetness of the morning dew
Shining on the blades of grass
I know you
As the blood which flows through my body
Carrying the force of life
I know you.

I Miss You

The current of the still waters of my soul
Runs deep with the thought of you.
Memories of your smile
Flow into the recesses of my heart
Living waters of your voice
Pour over the parched
Ears of my mind
Causing grass to grow
I hear sweet music
Drifting like mist
Rising from a waterfall
And yet I miss you so
Like a flame starved of living oxygen

Into the Night

Come with me my love, my life.
Come with me into the night.
Come run with me hand in hand
Naked in the still of the night.
Come let me find the secret pathway.
Come drink from the reed of life.
As I enter into the void of your night.
Wrap your self around me,
And fill my cup with your divine essence.
Fill my mouth with the wine
Which flows from the crown to the opened gate.
Come my Love, into the night
And as a love wraps his beloved about him
Then let us embrace the beauty of the night.

I Think of You

When poetry flow
Like a river wide
And thoughts
Like matchsticks
On the waves ride
I think of you and I smile

I Thought Of You Today

And these are the words
I wished I could say
As for you and me
We can not help but agree
That love does not change anyway
I hear your voice
And see your smile
In the sunshine everywhere
My yesterdays
And tomorrows hope
Are nothing when I am with you
Today

I Want to Find a Way

I want to find a way
To love you unquantified, unqualified
Spoken and yet not understood
Heard and yet not felt
For the medium absorbs the message
Floating in a bottle
On the river time
Waves rise and fall
And a boat drifts to
Unknown shores

I want to find a way
Back to you
For the edges of the envelope
Has been stretched anew

I want to find a way
That I could speak
And words would not get
In the way of all that I wished to say

I want to find a way
Or leave behind
Bread crumbs
Pointing the way
I hope to find

I want to find a way
That what I say
Is the same as what I do

And what begins with me
Will end with you.
I want to find a way

Journey

I have traveled,
Over oceans of time,
To be with you.
There has never been life,
When I,
Were not there with you.
Through countless lives
And different forms.
We have been together.
There is no possibility,
For me,
To love another.
I heard your call
From the depths of space
And in an instant
I am here.
There is no life
Or even death,
That can separate
Me from you.

Kiss Me

My mouth on yours
And all I can
Think of
Is the sound of two
Ripe red cherries
Falling on the ground
A kiss, long awaited
Breathlessly anticipated
Swimming in a sea
Of soft enclosures.
Two red dragons
Playing in a dark cave
Mouth open wide
Receiving something
Sweet and mysterious
Be silent
Be still.

Last Kiss

You offered me your lips of red
As I passed you by yesterday.
There along a deserted path
Upon the green grass you lay.
I pressed my lips
To the folds of you
And tasted the sweetness of morning dew.
I looked for you today
Wishing to see you as I pass
But how was I to know
That you were the type to kiss and go
And that kiss would be my last.
But of you I will remember this,
The sweetness of a hibiscus kiss.

Last Night

Last night I dreamt, I slept with you,
As we lay on our bed.
I gently touch your honeyed lips
With visions of love in my head.
For in my mind I'm safe with you,
Living in my dreams,
I'll use the cover of the night.
To walk inside your dreams,
Perchance to find you in the light,
A reflection on yonder stream.
I dread the sound of rooster's call,
The herald of the dawn .
The birth of light, the death of night,
The striking clock must fall.
The wheel must turn and come again,
To help us start anew.
I'll close my eyes and I will see,
You safely in my net.
The dreamer, dreams and so it seems,
That life is dream …and yet.

Let it Go

Oh, my father
Can you hear my cry
Oh, my father
My breaking heart
Cries flowing rivers.
Blood gushes
From the depths of my soul.
In twisted anguish
And subliminal pain
My soul
Lays desiccated
Like a winter's leaf
Freshly plucked from life's tree.
I listen for your voice
Through this torrent of pain
And all I can hear
Is but a whisper
A voice so soft
Which gently say
Let it go my son.
Let it go.
My son, let the love
You have for her,
Go.
Let it go my son.
Like the rising of the morning mist
Recedes in the approaching light.
Let it go.
Swift as an arrow
Sure as the sun,
Let your love for her go.
Let it go my son.

Like A Mist

Like a mist in the night
I will steal under your sheets
As a gentle evening breeze
I will wrap myself around you
I will whisper your name
To the lapping waves of the lake.
I will walk with you
Into the soft and gentle night
To that long forgotten place
Deep in the folds of creeping Time
We will travel on life's pathway
To leave footprints in the field of time.
My precious Love
Like a mist in the night
I will steal into your thoughts
As you float in the dreams of sweet remembrance

Looking for You

I lost my balance today
I went to the airport,
And you were not there.
I looked high and I looked low.
I had to stay,
I could not go.
I checked the board,
So many times.
It seemed as though,
I was losing my mind.
This was the first time
That I was scared.
For not seeing you there
Made me weak and afraid.
Although to me this feeling was new,
It is because I know that I love you.
Around you I'll place a fence,
In times of need or doubt.
I'll be your silent defense.
You will not have to shout.
I looked for you today,
And what did I find.
That you are strong,
In my heart soul and mind.

Love's Fire

If you are not consumed
By the fire of passion
Then you have not truly loved
If the love which beats
Within the sacred places
Of your heart
Is not fed by the stream
Of your last breath
Then how can you ever love
You must be consumed
By the flame of love
Love must be the force
Which ignites
The forge of your life.
Love goes beyond
The confines of description
And lives beyond emotion or passion.

My Lady

Have you seen this lady?
Yes?
Have you really seen this lady?
When you look at her,
Who do you see?
Crest of the wave,
Foam from the sea.
Is she wife, friend, or mother?
Plaything, prostitute, sister?
Do you see her as Other?
A crackling flame,
A burst of fresh air, feeding the fire.
Kiss her lips and draw her breath,
She is the giver of life,
The harbinger of death.
Deep within a cauldron boils,
From her hallowed womb,
A new life cries.
She opens her lips to speak,
On hearing the sound,
Your knees grow weak.
She is a trumpet playing,
Late in the night.
Her smooth and soothing notes,
Just makes it all feel right.
With a gently touch of her hand,
No need for words.
You'll understand.
Look not at this lady,
With the eyes of the blind.
But as a treasure that is hard to find.

Next Time

I will pour into your mouth,
Kisses like aged wine,
Like a swirling mist your scent,
I will keep, forever in my mind.
For I have been rescued,
From the perils of a love shipwrecked
And as you gently surrender,
I'll softly kiss your neck.
The sweet taste of your essence
Will be forever on my tongue
For within the confines of my soul
Is a place where you belong.
Oh! The sweetness of a stolen kiss,
A longing sigh, the state of bliss,
A parting whisper in my ear.
You leave,
I shed a silent tear.
Until the next time.

Morning Tea

Morning splashed across the sky
As I turn in my bed
My thoughts gently caress you.
I follow the contours of your face
And feel with my fingers,
The smile at the corners of your mouth
Your greetings of the day
Are silver on a small lake
In early spring
Dancing with the sunlight
As leaves waltz between light and shade.
It is wonderful to wake up with you
There is tea in the cup
And the mist which slowly rise,
Find its way to me
Ah! cinnamon, cherry or earl of grey
First light, second sight,
New day

Mundane Things

Mundane things enters my mind
Like what does your job entail?
And do you enjoy
A walk in the summer's rain
A glass of wine.
Or a book somehow
To pass the time and how.
Who are you?
And what makes you smile
Does the pain of
Life visit you for a while
So many questions
Knocks at the door.
Who are you now?
And who before.

My Anchor

In the midst of the storm of life,
When I am lost in foreign lands,
When I drift in a sea of uncertainty,
It's your voice that anchors me.

When desperation fills my mind,
While looking for answers, hard to find
You speak to me in that still small voice,
And open my mind and give me choice.

You are the rock, to which I cling,
A shelter from the winter wind.
A port to harbor from the storm.
And wings to cover me from harm.

With all my will I'll hold to you,
For you'll be there when my days are few.
With you I am sure of tomorrow,
For you are indeed my anchor.

My Treasures

These things I give to you.
The gold in the morning sun.
The joy in a full life's run.
The silver of the sea-side sand
And the line between yin and yang.
These things are my treasures.
I have nothing else to give to you,
Accept them my love,
In the spirit in which they are given.

One Goodbye

Overcast the afternoon sky
I sit here and wonder why.
So many miles,
Through clouds I fly.
There I must go,
There I will try.
There she stood,
As the cab pulled away.
So soft and broken,
No words to say.
A raised hand a silent goodbye.
I cannot look, for she will cry.
But I have promises to keep,
Tonight for me, there'll be no sleep.
I travel across the ocean wide,
To return like the rolling tide.
I'll leave you now to come again,
And be refreshed like falling rain.
Although the sky be overcast,
I know that this too will past.

One Song

Sing my love the one song
Sing of the germ of birth
The fecundity of the earth
And the glorious dance of death.

Sing my love the one song
Sing of a time and times half a time
The love of humans and of life
And the joy of ever-present strife.

Sing my love the one song
Sing of love and of the shadows
Of the length of thought
And the fullness of tomorrow.

Sing my love the one song
Sing of the touch of the body
And the warmth of an excited mind
And the wondrous joy of being alive.

One Thought

If I could have just one thought,
It would be one of you.
It would be one that's filled with love,
And kiss the morning dew.

A thought as wide as the ocean is deep.
The mountain's purple majestic peak.
The golden waves of harvest grain,
Spread far upon the Mara"s plain.

I wake with morning's light refreshed,
Of dreams and memories from a time of rest,
The new day opens like a window wide,
On wings of eagles my thoughts of you rise.

If I had but only one final thought,
Before I draw my last,
It will be of you my love,
My memory of the past.

Release Me

Out of the darkness of my dungeon I call.
From the depths of my soul I yearn for you,
To break these chains that bind me.
Oh! please release me.

Throw open the door of your heart,
And let slip your iron guard.
Let the hounds that stand guard,
At the gates of your soul sleep for a while.

Like a long lost lover I will steal,
Into you like a returning wind
Which flows through the crevices
Of a familiar old house.

Release me my love, and let me soar,
To bathe in the radiance of the sun
And caress the mountain tops
As they burst into the blue heavens.

My love, my life, let your tears of mercy
Fall on these my fetters.
Look on me a captive, a lowly slave
And release me.

Returning Home

Although you were the rock
Upon which the ship of my heart
Was wrecked.
I love you still
I thought of you as my anchor
In the storms of brutal separation.
Your love gave me a sure
And steady place.
To which I could return
But the line between you and I
Has stretched so far
That the way home is now lost.

Right Now

I am not feeling so tough, right now,
Maybe I've had enough, right now,
Never knew it could be so rough, right now,
Still I've got to be strong.

Feeling so alone, right now,
Looks like I can't go on, right now,
So far away from home, right now
Waiting for a sign.

We have drifted apart, right now,
So many stones in my heart, right now
How can we make a start, right now?
I will like to know.

I am bearing my soul, right now,
This story of us is old, right now
How can we make love unfold, right now
Come take my hand,

I am shedding my pride, right now,
To walk at your side, right now,
Laying my ego aside, right now
Look at this man.

I need to know, right now,
The way to make love grow, right now,
And though tears will flow, right now
Speak more than words.

All the time we have is, right now
No need to wonder, or even ask how,
To you this is my eternal vow,
Tomorrow is not promised, there is only right now.

Satin Sheets

The fire which burns within you
Makes your skin red to the touch
Shallow breath
Raising the hair on your neck
Bodies floating above the sheets
The interplay of flowing bodies
Coming and going
Like fishes at play.
Here a kiss, there a caress
Tense relaxation
Charges a perfumed atmosphere.
The sound of crashing waves
Beating upon the shore
A deep and powerful tide
Slowly rises inside
I feel you move
Against my skin
And I stop my breathing
My mind drinks deeply of you
Textures, taste, sights and sounds
All create a moving picture
Against the back drop
Of satin sheets.

Second Skin

My love when we touched
I was lost as to where to begin
I was so lost inside of you
That you felt like a second skin
The power and force of the emotion
Seizes my throat like a vice
And all the words I wished to say
Are now devoid of voice.
Like water flowing over,
Smooth and silky stones.
You cover me like a blanket
How can I ever feel alone?

Shattered Innocence

Should I My Love,
Break this mirror?
And watch the pieces
Of love fall to the ground.
Should I My Love
Suffer your silence
To be ruptured with the cry of Joy?
When you silently cry out.
I am yours and you are mine.
Should I my Love
Bend to the words of others?
Who in fear of life live in darkness.
Ignorant of the bliss of Love
As they lay trapped within a shell
Made with their own hands.
Should I my Love
Die of thirst
When the waters of life
Flow from the river of your lips.
To flood the plain of my tongue.
Should I My Love
Shatter the innocence
Of the sweetness of our love
Not born, yet filled with the germ
Of ripe potential.

Show Me the Face

Show me the face
You had before you met me
And I will show you mine
Speak the first word
Which shook the heavens
And proclaimed to all
I am that
Refresh my mind
Of the time
When you danced in the midst
Of swirling atoms
To the music of infinite space
Show me the life you lived
Before your mother was born
Or after your father swam across the sea
Didn't you know that
Stars fell from your eyes
And left holes in the curtain of the sky.
When I first saw your face.

Silent Waves

Silence,
Washes over me
Like the night,
Leaving memories of you,
Lingering in the shadows,
Like flotsam from a receding tide.
Darkness,
Like a misty blanket,
Comforts me.
And the absence of you,
Deepens my love,
Of you.
I listen in the stillness of my heart
For the sweetness of your voice,
And it washes over me,
In silence.

Small Diamond

Touch me
And let me pass
Through the narrow passage
Of your mind
Drops of sand
Like fiery planets
Fall into the black hole of time
The crush of naked reality
Leaves me cold and numb
Silent voices speak out in rage
Tears flow like molten lava
And yet the river flow
There is no rest.
The coal of my heart
Is crushed by raw emotion
Into a small diamond.

Soft as the Night

Soft as the night blows
Over the desert sands
Pure as the mountain dew
Heaven opens its window wide
In resplendent beauty
Angels flow through.
Like an ancient echo
Spoken long ago
A small seed was planted
And now it has begun to grow
No strange degree of wonder
Why does my heart beat so
It's for those same forgotten words
Spoken long ago

Speak Softly

Speak softly
Not to my ears
But to my heart
Listen gently
Not to the words
Which pour from
My mouth
But to the silence
Which hangs
Suspended like
Bridges from thought to thought
Touch me
With the intensity
Of one crossing
A knife-edged tightrope
Without a balance rod
Envelope me
With your mind
That it covers me
Like a second skin.

Still I Go On

There's a hole in my soul
Which only you can fill
We watch the dice roll
This time I might win

I have drawn from the well
And drunk deep every time
But my thirst was not filled
On this sweet October wine.

I will fill up my cup
With love from your stream
And pray from this dream
I may never wake up.

Silly little sweet rhymes
I will sing in your ear
To act as a magnet
To make our hearts draw near.

The touch of you
Is all that I seek
The feel of morning dew
On my bare naked feet.

No more silly little mind games
No more chasing around
For angels at times
Do walk on the ground.

Stillness of Your Voice

Let me not
See you as
You go.
Let me not
Hear your footsteps
As you walk away.
Let my body
Not starve
With the hunger
For your touch.
Let my lips
Not remember
The soft sweetness
Of your kiss.
Let the air
No longer reverberate
With the sound
Of your voice.
For my ears
Cannot bear to hear
The stillness of
Your voice.

Still Standing

Show me your heart
And I will show you mine.
Though scarred and broken.
Imprinted by the hand of time.
Through the valley,
Of death and desolation.
This poor heart has walked,
Surrounded yet in isolation.
This heart has seen,
The light of life
And held the hand of death.
Cut by words sharp as knife
Captured by shallow breath.
This heart has seen
The passion of a flower's smile.
And known the wink
Of the morning sun
As it stretches itself
Like a runner
Before his morning run.
A blade of grass
Comes to mind
As I search for an answer
Difficult to find.
The wind and rain
Both brought me pain
And yet I am still standing.
My heart though
Bowed and broken
Still stands.

Stolen Kiss

Oh the sweetness,
Of a soft and stolen kiss.
The trembling of a tender heart.
A loving look, a gentle gaze,
Lips slowly fall apart.
Emotions, like a swelling tide,
Cresting before the fall.
Primeval forces deep inside,
Rush to answer the call.
Oh, my soul which
I pour into this kiss
Is lost in rapture,
Filled with bliss.

Surrender

As the dawn surrender to the sun
My love surrender to me
Let me wrap you in the fire of my love
And be consumed by the flames.
In the desert of our desperation
I will be the water on your tongue
To quench your burning passion.
In your darkest hour I will be a flame
And when you are weary
I will fashion for you
A seat of stone.

Ten Thousand Years

Ten thousand years
Seems like yesterday since I last held you
Ten thousand years has passed
Since I last saw you
Ten thousand more to come
Karmic winds blow on the waters deep
Primordial slime awakes from its sleep.
Another life has begun.
Ten thousand years before I come.
Still, life sleeps in the womb of dark possibility.
The thunder clap and lightning strikes
Life is shaken from its slumber.
In the blinking of an eye.
Ten thousand worlds are created.
Another blink and ten thousand more die.
Ten thousand years will pass before
I hold your hand again.

Thank You

I thank you
For returning
The sunlight to my eyes
To see love's beauty.
I thank you
For opening
The door of my heart
That love may enter
I thank you
For pouring
Into a broken empty cup
The wine
Of your precious love
I thank you
For loving me
With the passion
Of your mind,
The tears of your soul
And the openness of your body.
I thank you
For taking this broken life
And making me whole
For the healing bliss
Of the oil which flowed
As the blessings
Of the midnight sun.
Causing rivers of cosmic streams
To forever run.
I thank you for giving voice
To words

Which danced upon the palate
Of a virginal page
And sang with the voice of angels.
I thank you
For being within the sound of my voice
And for answering the call.

The Fire

Last night, when we touched,
The fire torched the sheet,
But now in the light of day,
You pass and do not speak.
Oh! How the fire raged that night,
And consumed us like a storm.
The passion raced as a rushing tide,
And like the wind is gone.
My heart was in my fingertips,
And gently touched your spine.
I loved you not with body that night,
But with heart and soul and mind.
It seems that the fire,
Has scorched the very earth,
And changed the bed we lay upon.
And now it has given birth.
The fire is gone, and so the flame,
But the heat and the memory,
Will always remain.

The Dance

I'll take you in my arms,
And draw you close to me.
Deep within your eyes to look,
To see what's there for me.
A secret smile creeps o'er your lips
And silver lights your eyes.
A gentle stirring of the hips.
Soon stars fall from the skies.
I'll gently hold your hand in mine,
And caress the small of your back,
Taking several breadth of air,
To prevent this anxiety attack.
Softly I whisper, a small silent prayer
Oh God! Please do not let me make
Any mistakes today.
I'll run my fingers through your hair,
As you slowly come to rest,
My thoughts like untamed horses race,
Oh! My heart pounds in my chest
I want to dance with you,
A dance of life and love
To enter within your heart of hearts
As my fingers fits your glove
Although love for us is silent
Our hearts continue still
To beat to life's music
As the sun sets over the hill.

The Parting

My friend,
The time is here for the parting.
And although my heart is heavy.
Still, I must go on.
The pain of losing you,
Rips at my heart.
My tongue is silent, and my voice has deserted me.
Must I leave you now, at this time?
Is this adieu, or goodbye forever?
O! My friend how I fear leaving you.
O! How it pains me when my heart considers,
The need of you.
I am consumed with the flame for you.
My mouth is dry as the parched earth,
Oh do but quench the thirst of these my lips,
With the wine of your kisses.
Breathe into my mouth the breath of the morning,
That I will be refreshed for my journey,
Without you.
O! my friend let not our parting,
Be as an ending,
Rather let it be a new beginning,
Of things to come.

The Touch

There I was,
A fallen man.
Twisted and Broken
Unable to stand.
Then you came,
And touched my hand.
For that which
Once was dead.
By the touch,
Of your hand.
Is alive instead.
One could never think
That there was so much
In such a soft and simple
Touch.

This Beautiful Moon

I wish that you could see
The beauty in this moon.
I wish that you could hear
The music of the night
I wish that you could feel
The cool cover of its light
I wish that you could sing
This song of joyous life
I wish that you could dance
To the music of the rolling waves.
I wish that you could touch
The beauty of this loving night.
I wish that you could drink
From the essence of this life.
I wish that I could give
The beauty of this moon.
Like the petals of the opening Rose
I wish that you could stand naked.
And like a gentle breeze
I will enter your secret chamber.
All that I can do is wish
That I could give to you
This beautiful moon.

Together Forever

When you said that you will love me
I thought you meant forever.
When you said you will be with me
I thought you would leave me never.
You poured your words like honey
Dripping from the cone.
And with shallow bated breath,
I quickly followed you home.
My mind was filled with pictures,
Of images I should dread.
But it was made so easy
By the sheet which covered the bed.
I thought I knew my body
I thought I knew my mind
But the way you touched me.
Was like drinking from the vine.
The rise and fall of passion
The rising swelling tide.
The gentle knocking at the gate
And then you were inside.
My memory serves me all to well
Of a broken promise of forever
Which causes my tears to swell
For together is not forever.

Two Lovers

Two lovers kiss,
Between two parting lips.
Illusions and deception fade,
And truth is laid to rest.

Silent silver tears
Along a crooked path.
Trembling, empty, needy lips,
Words which still my fears.

Two weary hearts
Worn out souls,
Along life's winding path,
At last two lovers meet.

Unbroken Wall

If there were
A way
Or word
That I
Could speak
To break
This wall
Of silence.
Such a word
Would shake
The foundations
Of heaven.
And
Like raging storms
Bursting with emotions
Straining at the boundaries
Of expression.
Wash away all
In its path.

Unspoken Words

These are unspoken words,
I wished I could say.
How the sound of your voice,
Do take my breath away.
Or that the smile on your face,
Can cause my heart,
To quicken its pace.
Or how I am intoxicated
By the smell of you,
And how it lingers,
Long after you are out of my view.
In the storeroom of my mind
There is an image of you.
Filled with warmth and radiant sunshine.
These feelings overwhelmed me today,
And if I had the words
This is what I wished I could say.

What Might Have Been

When like a gentle rolling wind
You flow across my mind
I think of what might have been
And like a piece of stale dry bread
You become stuck in my throat
I am unable to swallow
And I choke,
On what might have been.
Haunting thoughts
Ghosts of potent possibilities
Possess my soul
I am become
That which is lost between
What might have been
And what should've been.
Thoughts of tomorrow
Go begging in the streets of yesterday
Timeless echoes in the halls of
What might have been.

Words

If I,
Could be so bold.
To use the spoken word,
And open a window
To your soul.
But words,
Though soft and sweet.
I see them now,
Like discarded sonnets,
Lying at your feet.
Perhaps they are the remains,
Of those who suffered,
Thinking that love ferments
Through the wine of pain.
Or maybe like familiar echoes
They are.
Returning like distant memories from afar.
Oh, these empty words,
You have heard before,
And yet some fool
Still knocks at your door.

Yesterday

Yesterday came,
And your face
I did not see.
Yesterday came
And my pain
Was there for all to see.
Yesterday came,
And the sweetness
Of your smile
Did not grace your face
Yesterday came,
And the cup of wine
Had lost all its taste.
Yesterday came,
And my thirst
Went unquenched.
For there was no kiss.
Yesterday came,
And it was then
I knew that love
Was made of this.
Yesterday came,
And the song
Of your voice
Was silent in my ears.
Yesterday came,
And my heart
Was once again
Swept away by tears.
Yesterday came,

And it went,
Unfinished and empty.
There was no you.

You Don't Have To

You don't have to love me
For to expect this,
Will be too much.
But if we can walk along,
Life's rocky road
And still be there at its end
Then it's enough.
You don't have to shine,
Like the sun in my life.
Just bring a candle,
In the dead of night.
There is nothing,
That you must do.
Life is all simplicity,
Its essence flows through
You and me.
It raises its forms,
On the morning tide,
And lays them down,
At evening time.
You don't have to.

About the Author

Originally from the Caribbean, KASANTI™ is an Ordained Minister, a student and teacher of the martial arts and a Buddhist. He took the name KASANTI™ on his ordination. It is derived from Sanskrit "Ksanti" (power of Patience).

KASANTI™'s poetry shows influences from his travels and having been exposed to different cultures. KASANTI™ is spiritual and his poems certainly reflect a view of life through the eyes of someone to whom nature has blessed with second sight. KASANTI™ cares a great deal about the world. His writings are more than just a way of expressing his feelings; it is a way for him to share his concerns and his hopes for the world. KASANTI™ has the talent for putting thoughts on paper in such a way that cause you to ponder and contemplate. In sharing these poems which presented themselves to him, it is hoped that they resonate and perhaps act as sign posts along the way.

KASANTI™ is more than a poet; he is an activist and a strong proponent of human rights. He has focused his efforts on the provision of access to primary education.

Printed in the United States
45175LVS00002B/28-228